THE
PURITAN
CARPENTER

by

Julia Randall

The University of North Carolina Press · Chapel Hill

1965

CONTEMPORARY POETRY SERIES

Copyright © 1961, 1962, 1964, 1965 by Julia Randall Sawyer

"The Company" and "The Coast" originally appeared in *Poetry*.
Other poems in this volume have been published in *The Sewanee Review,
The American Scholar, The Johns Hopkins Magazine,* and *The Hollins Critic*.

Library of Congress Catalog Card Number 65-23137

*Printed by The North Carolina State University Print Shop, Raleigh
Manufactured in the United States of America*

FOR LOUIS RUBIN

Whose furious motion

astonishes us all

CONTENTS

THE
PURITAN
CARPENTER

ROCKLAND

Masters, be kind to the old house that must fall,
Burn, or be bulldozed. The apples have grown small
And the ivy great here. The walk must be moved once
        more
Beyond the holly. Do not use the side door,
The lilies have broken the step. If you fix it,
They will break it again; they live under the stone.
There is blown glass
In three windows; hold them up with a stick.
The smoke is always thick
With the first fire. The Landseer in the attic
Was tacked there when I came. There is a snake
With a red tongue in the terrace; he has never been
        known
To hurt. The worst leak
Is in the bedroom ceiling. So. It was a good house
For hands to patch, a boon to August eyes. And when
The moon lay on the locusts, and the stream
Croaked in the bottom, muted by high grass,
Small rustlings in the woodlot, birdcries, was
A minister like music. Should I say
This—with the apple tree—was Sirmio,
This—with the two-year parsley—Twickenham,
Aldworth, or Abbotsford, I would only mean
We lease one house in love's divided name.

THE MAN ON THE PARKING LOT

The man on the parking lot
Is some sort of cripple, not
That he limps or hasn't his eyes:
I know when I hear his voice
Cry Lady! Lady! with more
Urgency than the police.
It is hoarse like a dog with rage
Against my human shape.
I roll the window up
Instinctively; he is right
There, snarling at the glass.
This week, like the week before,
I am in the wrong space.

I am only going to buy
Beer. It is Saturday.
They have locked the Union Trust;
The lot is virtually empty.
But which is Robinson's spot?
It didn't rain in September;
Then it was by the door.
All the sloppy weather
It was about as far
Away as you could get
By the uncleared exit.
Now he is screaming me down
To the Battery Service Wall.
There has never been a sign.

He has an ugly will
This Cerberus. I accept
The scutcheons of the Law
Which shine for all to see:
The traffic must move smoothly.
Take Martin Chenowith.
I had at least three tickets
From him in the mythic past.
In fear of God and Father
I scrounged five dollars from
My small, unlicensed brother

And took it humbly in
To the station-house in person,
Grateful that I could pay
For silence and regulation.
Now the old eagle bows
To me, at my moneyed house,
Where he keeps the swinging door,
Un-uniformed, old, poor,
But kind as he always was
Behind the imposing laws.

I do not seek excuse.
I could give up beer,
Or change my liquor store.
I could lock the car
And leave it. I could force
The dog of the Union Trust
To his superiors.
I could make endless wars.
And yet, and yet
It moves me like a game,
Though I have never been right,
And sometimes my teeth are set
All the way home
In anger or fear or both;
Though the monstrous guardian
Pursues me in a dream
Around the drive-in booth.
Does he keep the vaulted dead?
Am I seeking to get in
Or stay out? How do I win?
I have certainly missed my slot.

But next and next week, led
By rote, or temerity,
It will be Lady! Lady!
Lady! around the lot
Where I will never fit

The mongrel lies at ready.
My Sunday beer is sweet.

TO WILLIAM WORDSWORTH FROM VIRGINIA

I think, old bone, the world's not with us much.
I think it is too difficult to see,
But easy to discuss. Behold the bush.
His seasons out-maneuver Proteus.
This year, because of the drought, the barberry
Is all goldflakes in August, but I'll still say
To the First Grade next month, "Now it is Fall.
You see the leaves go bright, and then go small.
You see October's greatcoat. It is gold.
It will lie on the earth to keep the seed's foot warm.
Then, Andrew Obenchain, what happens in June?"
And Andrew, being mountain-bred, will know
Catawba runs too deep for the bus to get
Across the ford—at least it did last May,
And school was out, and the laundry wouldn't dry,
And when the creek went down, the bluebells lay
In Hancock's pasture-border, thick as hay.

What do they tell the First Grade in Peru,
I wonder? All the story: God is good,
He counts the children, and the sparrow's wing.
God loved William Wordsworth in the spring.
William Wordsworth had enough to eat.
Wye was his broth, Helvellyn was his meat,
And English was his cookstove. And where did words
Come from, Carlyle Rucker? Words that slide
The world together. Words that split the tide
Apart for Moses (not for Mahon's bus),
Words that say, the bushes burn for us—
Lilac, forsythia, orange, Sharon rose—
For us the seasons wheel, the lovers wait,
All things become the flesh of our delight,
The evidence of our wishes.

                              Witch, so might
I stand beside the barberry and dream
Wisdom to babes, and health to beggar men,
And help to David hunting in the hills

The Appalachian fox. By words, I might.
But, sir, I am tired of living in a lake
Among the watery weeds and weedy blue
Shadows of flowers that Hancock never grew.
I am tired of my wet wishes, of running away
Like all the nymphs, from the droughty eye of day.
Run, Daphne. Run, Europa, Io, run!
There is not a god left underneath the sun
To balk, to ride, to suffer, to obey.
Here is the unseasonable barberry.
Here is the black face of a child in need.
Here is the bloody figure of a man.
Run, Great Excursioner. Run if you can.

A SCARLET LETTER ABOUT MARY MAGDALENE

If I asked you to look out
The back window, where the crumbs are spread,
And asked you who was king
Of the sparrows, you would say the red
Bird, not a sparrow, and not because
He has manners, or is larger than them all.
He is not more virtuous:
He is more beautiful.

It is hard to conceive
A god irrational as man,
But we believe
In the image, patch it as we can.
We fall in love
Not with the best or brightest in the nest
Of reason, but some light in the heart's cave.

And that, perhaps, my dear, is how we save
Ourselves. How after a life of sin,
We say "I love you," and we enter in
Unworthy, to the kingdom which he made,
Where weak are strong, whores maid,
And oily love announces: I obeyed
Necessity, who blessed me.
God possessed me.

FOUR FEARFUL SONGS

1.

Harsh birdsong is best. The thrush is sweet
And the dove's echo from the willowy moonlot.
Sparrows dissent
And thrive, inelegant, in dirty eaves
And vines tougher than brick. The sea,
Sickened by whispers, keeps the famished gull
For music.
    Far from hell
Is best. Where cries are thickest,
There no nightmare
Deafs the dreaming ear. Crow, jay,
Chattering pie, protect us from the voice
Of the dead, distract us from
Their door. Good mocker, cry
Company, company, from the blackest bough.

2.

Better a rock than quicksand. Better a spine
Than a garden pit. Untangle me, green vine.
Where the ivies creep, soon, soon the sucking sun
Will have the leaves of my heart. Only a mountain
Stands in his bones. He cracks the seasons small.
His ruin is the soft sky's fall.
Till then, be flint, my rickety animal.

3.

I creep wherever I go. I crowd my eye
With granite flecks and grains of mulberry.
I practice grass,
That blade and hair and hue,
Kernel and sap of me,
Fallen upon their peace
May recognize the place.

4.
My stormy eyes at sleep
Fill up the graves with light.
My heart lying down
Bloods ghosts to rise and walk.
I lent a child my tongue
And kept my father's ear.
"You cannot live alone," they sang,
"Nowhere, nowhere.
The waters that turn the earth,
The fire that turns the sky
Bloody a man's birth
And light his dreaming eye,
Light eagle and cornblade,
Apple and shell and stone,
And lit god's dreaming eye
That could not sleep alone."

A WINDY KERCHIEF

I saw a windy kerchief
Ravelling on a bough.
Sun and rain together
Made a ragged show.
Some head must bear the weather
Or bind itself anew.

There went Lancelot
Tasselled as a clown,
Weeping through Almesbury Wood
For his great love and sin.
He put his bonnet off
And died a holy man.

But how the great gods went
In feather, hoof, and fire!
Every lineament
Outfitted in desire:
Gold limb, feathery gaudiness,
Then beauty bare.

BOUNDBROOK

I met a man and he was fair.
All the birds said Follow.
Every leaf in the wood
Shook gold onto my head
And my heart felt all its blood.

Then it was a great park land
By a willow-trailing brook bound round.
Stag and peacock walked
For pleasure in the corn,
And Merlin wound the horn.

Merlin or his tribe it was
Spun that park and lordly palace
Pearled as Helen's pin.
My master said, Walk in,
And, Touch me. It is yours.

I had a hand could change a world.
The waters dropped, the meadow furled,
That field was Circe's pen.
The shaggy beasts growled at the shucks,
Great swine, and goats, and picking cocks,
And they were all my kin.

Seven years I sojourned there,
The blacksnake nested in the briar,
Every bird was black.
Insects stained the air like smoke.
I struck and ravined in the thick
Until my heart's blood broke.

And I lay down, a beast, to die
And rose up seven years ago
In the poplar fields of home.
There the streams go out and in,
All the men are common men,
The blackbird whistles in the corn.
Touch me. It is mine.

AN ALTARPIECE

A light, but not the sun's, streams on the book
My lady reads, a Latin tale, her own,
Where lilied Gabriel bends, as in the room,
Foredreamed, he kneels among
Neat towels, pewter, and the songster's cage
Till he repeat the tidings on the page:
Blessed art thou.
              Outside, in the noonday village,
The bells, prepared, strike what he smiles to tell
On brick and cobble. I am Gabriel
In Brussels. In a room apart,
An old man whittles traps to catch the sins
That creep by night, when bells sleep, and the breast
Where doves have settled, while the studio dust
Settles upon the day's work.

Angel, maid,
And man, where do they dwell? Blue over rose—
Where is the tissue woven that shall clothe
Gretchen immaculate, wrap weeds in light,
Make words to speak all welcome? Old
Announcing masters, tell my ear, my eye.
My house is noisy, and from the street
The traffic voices cry my quiet book
To syllables that knock about my head
And will not set. Compose me, Rogier, Jan,
Apprentice me to listen till I fit
Small Gretchen's shriek to music, and hear plain
The carpenter's boy sing in the lettered hymn,
That like the maid whose candle has gone out,
I read and smile, but by another light.

COME, KILL ME CLEANLY

Come, kill me cleanly.
Chafing pities
Bind my breast;
My gut in stitches
Cramps; my crutches
Call new harpies in my way;
My blood seeps cruelly.

Cancel me, let me breathe
The long mechanical dark.
Love that has no stop
Curses the tongue in the teeth,
The marrow that makes the bone,
The nerve that shakes the dream,
The cripple that wakes in his room
Remedied of death.

THE COMPANY

And Yeats may dine at journey's end
With Landor and with Donne
And all irascible scribbling men
Who put such passion on
For Helen's honey-banded brow
And the iron-browed God of heaven
Their hearts grew thick upon the pain
And toughened, until now
They pump a more than mortal balm
Upon our sores, and sing us calm.

Let a woman take a fool to bed
And put a poet by;
Let God take children to his throne.
There is a devil in a man
Whose luck it is to cry
On beauty never quite possessed,
On quiet where the soul has rest
From endless fantasy.

Those syllables that substitute
For hand in hand, or eye to eye,
Will find no harp in heaven.
And yet your music shall be sweet,
Brave gentlemen, when poets meet
Who are the peers of time,
Who speak into its longing ear
What grace we might, what gifts we have.
Then, then love leaps the imperfect grave
To consummation, here.

THE FARMER'S TALE

Farmer, farmer, tell me,
My crop is slow to make,
Your wagon goes to market
Seven days a week.

You've melon for your daughter
And berry for your son.
Now by the rain that falls the same,
Why have I none?

Because the rain is equal,
Because the seed is true,
It is not every husbandman
His pulse and pastures grow.

Who sows a marble acre
Six of his seeds will die,
Let him hoe and shelter,
Let him weep and pray,

Let him shield the seventh,
Though market be there none,
Neither maize nor melon,
Neither daughter nor son.

There comes a lusty flower,
But rare, rare.
I cannot tell the color
But people at the Fair

Recall a ruined farmer
Who danced upon a stone
Until it bore that wonder,
The glory of the town,

The envy of the country.
But none could buy that bloom.
He flung it to the farmer's boy
And struck up harvest home.

A THEME OF HERBERT'S

Let me not know you if I do not know
All brightness sullies in the weather's eye,
All dreams are patches on old Plato's coat,
But ghosts pipe music when we walk in clay,
And when we mix there's magic in the flute.

Let me not serve you if I do not serve
Your praise, your honor, your great need or small.
Fond heads protest their passion to the grave,
Which exacts little, knowing ears alive
Will hear them all expert and dutiful.

Let me not love you if I do not love,
Beyond all other dances in the sun,
To match the time your feet make when they move
In any space. And should you walk alone,
Want nothing, or want nature clean forgot,
Let me not love you if I love you not.

HIGH ASWAN

Lord Ramses sailed upon
His father's lake,
Ruby at wrist and crown,
Gold at his neck;
Sheets the color of dawn
Flushed rush and brake;
Woodwind and sweet sistrum
Untuned that lake.

"He builds a temple,
Kheta's bane,"
Said the wild heron.
"Nubia's sun
Shall do his bidding
Year on year.
I have but a feather
For his steed's ear."

Sons at his feet
Breed many a son;
The horse and the rider
Shall part the stream,
And the chariot wash
When the seas return.

THE COAST

How, arriving from any waste,
The heart leaps to the guiding coast.
Without the eyes' assurance
Even our instruments and natural talents
Are poor props in the random troughs
Of hills and waters. Crest on crest,
Planet on planet tries the chart of space.
Even savage rocks,
After plains passed or surf run,
Miles of the sluggish river, years of stars,
Even the rocks' rude direction
Settles our task. There will be dunes to cross,
Cliffs, entering bays. But north, south, east, or west,
Their line sets out a continent, bounds a home
For inland exploration.
                                        May I return,
Thus, from the wilds of absence, where I lose
Feature, being one with all the elements,
Wave with the drifted wave, or light in air,
Blown seed with seed, straight to the edge and center
Of all my maps, my saving break in space,
My love: not Caribee to Columbus
Gives better name, or locates wandering faith
More sure than the wished-for dangers of your face.

A YOUNG SQUIRREL DEAD

The beast whose sudden fall
Was not a grief, whose birth, without a plan,
Was a brief pain,
Tells me how love lives in a name.

Already I see you lean
In the doorway, saying to put joy down
At your safe return
That was not to me. If I were a sane
Whole animal, I would strike and so compel
Submission without shame, or I would go
Scurrying away, drop joy like a nut
And find another out, welcome when met,
But unborn out of sight.

But no,
Alone in a patch of August I make this joy
For the winter, like a sun that will belie
The shrinking light, like a beast that cannot die
Of a mere block in nature. Oh never until I
Shape my mouth for death, and practice how
The breath will stop, so, never will this bough
Break and permit my honest flesh to fall
To a peace so neat, a bed so literal.

MARYLAND

True, there are other places more
Comfortable for the climate. If one lives
By one's skin, there is always California. By one's eye,
An Alp, or the distant prospect of the Bay
Of Salerno from the Belvedere
Cimbrone (where one can also die
Of the heat). But it is not that. One takes
The sun as it comes (provided it comes)
Quite naturally. There are fans,
Swimming pools, sprinklers, screens, and bug
Bombs. Even the sycamore
Has been known to stir, and locust in August storms
Cracks. As one takes
Sumac, ailanthus, mulberries on the sill,
The cornflower, the whippoorwill (this is the first year
I have seen an oriole south of New Jersey),
Tomatoes and tobacco. Not one rare
Peculiar thing, except the Naval Academy, or the great
Dilapidated hospital: Come to me,
Ye disconsolate foreign princes, blue babies from
Georgia, and Bill and Van,
Every Saturday night, from Wolfe Street. And I will
    give you
Pigeons, watermelon, Edgar Allan
Poe, the Star Spangled
Banner,
And the Carrolls, Howards, Ridgelys, Warfields, Blairs,
Whose beaming swords were turned into ploughshares,
First, then Georgian mansions, and gray stone farms
For the younger brothers; now for all, for all,
The golf course, the shopping center, and the Foxhall
Homes of distinction. As if every village
Did not have heroes, born, adopted, dead,
Buried, or partially buried (when the head
And heart lived separate). You are approaching
Hillsboro, New Hampshire, the birthplace
Of President Franklin Pierce. And in the ex-Convento,
Amalfi, the lettered memory of

Enrico Wadsworth Longfellow, very far
From Gitchee-Gumee, and the styles of snow
On Brattle Street.

No, it is not the local habitation—
Cedars by white-washed fences, some half gone
With honeysuckle. And not Chesapeake, the name.
No, it is knowing them somehow for one's own,
Environs of the single history
That matters, and a force in it. Thus,
One could wear sneakers on the rue de
Rivoli, but never on Charles Street, for they look,
Those doctors' offices, and those sad apartments,
The Sheraton-Belvedere, and those purveyors
Of reproduction antique furniture,
They look with Grandmother's eyes, and they carry the
     news
Home to one's conscience. Or say that one should meet
Mrs. Lenhart in Cleveland. One would say "How dull,"
And be right. But in the A & P
At Roland and Deepdene, one somehow remembers
Those who were nice to Father, those who sent
A bouquet at graduation, those whose sons
Are missing since Korea, those who fix
Clocks, those who know the recipe
For cucumber aspic.

Somewhere, Sir Thomas Browne,
In a friend's face, dying, saw a ghost of bone
Rise, and the family feature
Clear off the curves of earned, familiar nature:
Lusts, comforts, every lineament of school,
Or private light of industry or travel.
Pure Peter vanished, and the patient lay
Pure Willoughby, pure Cameron, family clay
Startled to reclamation. Then if place,
Too, is our ancestor (that is
The forever England concept), this low east,
Like love, rides in the gesture of my flesh.

Green Appalachian must outlast
Apennine or Sierra—even the sun
That struck on Shasta while we ate
Lunch, and the hoary marmots watched, or even
Dust on that mountain steeper than the way
From Lerici to Turbia. Cardinal
Cannot turn nightingale, wisteria come
Hawthorn or oleander, nor I root
Far from Patapsco's ledges, or Wye's foot.

MAID'S SONG

I wept on cypress knees,
I made a coat of moss,
I took the glowing worm
And hid him from the grass.

The river moved but once,
I could not plant my foot,
I'd mouths about my arm.
At last my love went out.

SCIENCE AND POETRY: THREE COMMENTS

1.

To grate the greenness of the green
Is not, mynheer, to desecrate
The grail of crusted artistry
Whose fictive emeralds wink as bright.

We two set forth from Camelot:
The analytic with his board
To bare the essential animal,
And you, my unaccoutred bard,
Describing sounds of hoo and ha,
And jigging at resemblances.

Our strategies, mynheer, diverge,
But Joseph keeps the chapel warm,
And curious questers up and down
Spy out the samite mysteries.

Record, doktor. And fool, jig on.

2.

The moon that was our mystery
Is that pocked orb and weary ash.

But who, careening in borrowed light,
Questions the cinder's potency?

As if the new geography
Were parenthetic to our scheme—

As if, occasionally, one caught
Echoes of actual Artemis.

3.

There is no limiting of the blue
That leaps above the blue beyond.
There is the unwillingness to look

Over the frosty burdock's head
In this December floor of light.

In this December floor of light
As if the shimmering twig were all,
And dull that pierceless cupola.

So dull that pierceless cupola,
Imagination flaked beneath:
As if the gods themselves were cast
In moods of ours to icy death.

FOR A HOMECOMING

I wish you were not flying, and I wish
Women were not fond, and men were not foolish.
Who'd ever invent
Wings out of wax, that had godsent
Patience-plumes to plumb her element?
Safe in my space, and surfeited, I stare
At the new violence in the air,
And think of little boys who screw the tops
Off the cleaning fluid, and knot the heads of mops,
And peel the bark off trees, and kick the stones
When there's no one around to pester with questions.
Oh, I know,
I'd be content in a cave, and I know that some
Incredibly curious germ of evolution
Lets you conceive a rafter and a beam
And a plastic tablecloth. A single name
Is all my woe, whatever was first on the tongue
In the beginning. Disaster and joy came then
Honestly: a banana was not a storm,
Absent was over, present was, possibly, warm.
But oh the daisy-petal words: is not,
Is or is not, is safe, tired, hungry, sick,
Unfaithful, lost, laughing, will not come home,
Will come home late. I will not sleep all night,
Preparing the news, hearing the morning break
In the trees, and the wings unfold that cannot make
Any but natural journeys while they wake.

MIRACLES

I said to the stream, Be still, and it was still.
I walked across the water like a fool.
Such ease—you'd think a man had never tried
The simple miracles, but lived and died
Sweating at wood and steel: chop, forge, bend, bind,
Get up the armory, don't trust humankind,
They were damned from the start.

                              I said to the mineral hill,
Lie down, and the hanging rocks and the canyons fell
As soft as smoke. It was quiet. I called out
Some friends to look. For a while they walked about
Uncomfortably, I thought, and one picked up
A fragment for the Museum. Envy? Fear?
I don't know what. I kept on all that year.
Wherever I went, the trees bowed down; the fruit
Rolled like obedient coins to my feet,
And so on. Late one night I tried to command—
How shall I say?—my holy spell to end,
Break, blast, unmagic me here in the dark
Tower I'd built. I wanted a horn to knock
The cullis in, and the crazy ditch to rise.
Oh god, for the need of nails, for the wild eyes
Of Noah with creation in his hold
Stampeding. But I'd sold
My Ararat for meadows. Oh, the flowers!
Too deep, too deep.
I said, accept my tears.

STYGIAN

I had heard in my youth
Of the water that bound the earth
Like a supple, fatal beast
With his tail in his mouth,
Immense and circular.
I never stopped to fear
The little bending creeks,
Susquehanna's arcs,
Or the turns of Delaware,
Till last night when I came
To the ford at Coldstone Gap.
I saw a serpent's eye
Glint in the running light,
And held one foot in air
And one on the crossing rock.
Something was dead on the shore.
I did not stop to look
But took Catawba's wall
And shouted coming over
To Craig and Newcastle,
"I have crossed the world's river!"

FOR T. R., 1908-1963

Lurcher from Genesis, long man of light,
Maker past making, beggar crippled back
Past crying alms of earth or alms of air,
I cannot reach you in the near field where
Your cells ungather darkly on their ways
To mine and bloom and all the million bodies
Time chances for the homing of its play.
The nameless need no comfort; it is we
Cry brother, brother to the witless grass,
And ghostly from the flesh of all that was
The first voice sings that turned the deep to day.

When monstrous and unorthodox you lay
Mouth open to the moss and called it kin,
Unearthed the crooked meat beneath the stone,
Went fish-ways, eyed the breather in the slime,
Or up, sat up not hay-high in your fur
To stop the vireo and freeze the weather,
All kind religions faltered. What is man
If his chief good and market in his time
Is feeding lips and bones dropped down to root?
You said, time was before my bones stood up,
Time was before my tongue, formed in the dark,
Sang him together for a dwelling-place.
His pyramids of sleepers are my house,
His planets are the fire-fields where I walk
Befriended into waking.

                              Journeyman,
Come ride me now a little into green,
You and your company. In my low air
A patient music moves, as of the light
Gathered in leaves, and I, a gatherer
Of void intimations, make this shape
For you to live in, and I know not what
Children to cradle shell-like at their ear.
It's blood alone, the wise men say, they hear.

Loud blood it is, and running on the bone,
Builds griefs and muscled pleasures of its own,
But secret brings the sea, secret the land
Limned out for love, where every bone shall stand
Stiff in the fellowship of the first word
That spoke man, mineral, petal, minnow, bird.

My Ariel sings like Haydn.
Prosper me, good grace.
I am all loss
Now, in this island of my winter house,
Son, brother, lover dreamed of, done.
The moon looks out as never a storm
Had bruised her blind, unmagicked eye.
The telltale snow
Shows ghastlier now.

How many fathoms fell the rain?
Will that music come again?
The queen my mother drowned before.
I know the taste of sea-water.

Sweet guide, restore my neighborhood
With day. Make all dreams fade,
Especially the good. I had once pearl eyes
And coral bones and sea-cut palaces.
But Ariel, Ariel, I could not kiss!

AN EXPEDITION

to the upper branches of James River to discover
gold or the South Sea was made, but neither was
found.

—Kegley's *Virginia Frontier*

Getting there is not hard. You must be provided,
Of course, with a charm. Something like an old blanket,
Good enough for the children to play house with,
If that's what they're doing. If it isn't a poem
Of magic carpets, soaring beyond home:
Soiled wool the track itself, the vehicle,
The welcome cave, the sleeping skin of love.

So. Piedmont is good, but the home of the brave
Seems further from the lawn, perhaps through the
      wood,
Up a bit, where the snakes live, up a bit
Where the waters break and dwindle, running down
To the sea we have lost the sound of, somehow.
Corn we remember, being hungry. Fire
We remember from the red oak, frond and term.
Is this snowdrop or snow? I have missed the season;
Remember, however, an Easter when snow came
And we couldn't get to the station.
I say a name loud: James, my father. Eagle Rock
Makes plain the mountains up to Iron Gate,
And every pair engendering a slot
To give the waters room.
I am tired. I will lie down.
Come find me in my blanket. When I am big,
I will know this range, I will see where the streams
      start,
Follow them over where the seasons go,
To the west, to the west. They will ask me what I am
      after.
Gold, I will say. Say, Beulah. The South Sea.

VARIATIONS: THE PURITAN CARPENTER

1.

I gave my love a scarlet cloak,
But dun he dyed it, skirt and yoke.
I gave my love a dancing tune,
But he went marching on and on.

I gave my love a world to live
Without a gibbet or a grave,
But such a carpenter was he,
He built the coffin and the tree.

2.

I do not dance, I do not sing.
Quiet on a weekday morning,
With a candle and a broom
I set to rights my single room:
Rind to larder, rug to bed,
Book to time, and dream to need.

I do not run, I do not stop.
The compass of my hall is sweet:
Log to winter, air to May.
Even years spare me and serve me.

> Strawblood, dancing on a line,
> Have you passions of your own?

3.

I too have built a house,
Muscle and nerve and bone
Gray as mason's dust,
Have fitted mortar and stone,
Fitted stone and mortar
Against the plunging moon
And her bitter weather.

Any port from storm,
Fortress or pleasure-dome
Over the caves of ice
Or the sacred river.
Who takes the raging sun?
None, since Adam's eye
Looked naked on his own
Bald and staining body.

I shall be dressed to die.

4.

Come, build a cage for the mind,
Set it water and meat,
That else would rage through the night
With honey and gall to eat,
And bruise its travelling feet
On the mountain-tracks of desire:
Wind's horn, rock's spine,
Rain's cup, October's tinder.

I count a little square,
Pallet and hewn trough,
Where the light comes quiet,
World enough, world enough.

5.

Keep the hawk blind,
Keep the dog chained.
The limb unleashed
And the unleashed mind
Grow tame and easy,
Easy and tame
Learning the wind
That shifts the sun
From crag to lawn,
Lawn to tree,
Over and over again
Learning the small rain.
But for the war

On the trespasser
Of earth or air,
For the clean kill
At the nerve's edge
And the belly full,
Keep the eye down
From comfort, fierce
From the brain's caul,
From the blood's noose.

6.

You will never trace me
In the bedevilled dew.
Cloak and staff in my entry
Summer and winter through
Hang well-pegged. For the Hangman
Will come. I shall be ready,
Booted and brushed, still new
For my wedding journey.

7.

If you should force my entry
In the night,
And crack against my posts, groping for light,
And pain of light sprung on the feeling blind,
I did not deal the murder. Like your kind,
You magicked in the old spell of the moon,
Poor lanterned worm, that could not light to bed
A millet grain. You kindled and you bled
Of that false fire, the cinder in the seed.
Make me no cry.
You ran upon the dagger. You will die.

8.

Be strict, my dear, and stony,
And lock away my sins,
And you shall have a peaceful house
And quiet for your pains.

There is a peace of marble things,
Noble head and eye,
Mountainous, maybe—Everest,
Each of his seasons snow.

And then the dearer innocence:
Cold acres come to corn,
Such unpretentious monuments
As common pilgrims earn.

9.

Before the frost has eaten
The crude remaining berry,
Fools see May in the tree
And the jewelled horn of plenty.

I have seen the hearts climb
Like crazy saps, and hang,
Trinkets of a season,
Until they are culled, flung,
Parched, consumed, or rotten;
Every sun the same
Rinse of gaudy hope.

Of cypress heart I made
Bench, table, and bed,
A floor to cripple the root,
A wall too smooth to suck,
And a roof to keep the shade.

In a room without a pulse
I practice for my peace.

10.

I temper as I would
The seasons of my voice,
Make dew of iron rust,
And jessamine of ice.

I say I will not bear
August her sheaf, September
Her vine; rather among
Gravels go barren.

Unlearned of all heat,
Like stones, without a root
Or turgid stem, I sing
Against false spring.

11.
High over the sea town,
Stone against the sky:
Shut love in a dark tower,
Love will die.

Like a child by the seashore,
I am foolish grown
Raising wall and turret
To watch them drown.

Mine is a sandy spirit,
Incapable of iron.

12.
Farewell my love, and well my love
To sweep your garden clean,
For dock and crab grow thickest
Where marigolds have been.

Gravel your plot, and contemplate
An oriental span.
Rock is its own magnificence;
I keep my armour green.

FIGURE

Light has no shape, but as it falls
Now on the mulberry, now on the rose,
Or creeps on grass.
Dark has no danger, but it takes
The depth of water, or the rock's
Plunge or foot-place.
So I move
To take some figure, or dissolve
Some face, some limb in shapeless love.
But you, by reason,
Bold as a winter oak, mark out
Acre and entranceway, and make
Shape of the season.

VARIATION

Song sharpened, city built,
Field sown, by note, by spire,
By seed upon the air
Cast in, cast out.

Twin towers at Koln the city,
And one is gone by fire;
Thrice are my fields at harvest,
Brian's thrice fallow.

Lilo dances in heaven,
Merodis' feet are stone;
White fingers at the lute
Construct, eliminate.

Notes reach into choir
Over notes at rest;
Blind Harry's harp is broken
Who sang best.

A POSTCARD FROM ASSISI

Come now to die
In the long corner where the saints
Stir up the lost kingdom of God's mercy,
Here I cry
All my loves' names in the teeth of the fiery dark
Till angels quench me and clouds rape
The holy breath of my last human shape.

I will quiet for this: to silence all my foes,
Commissioned when the waters and the lands
Gathered, the unseen work of unseen hands
That set division in the firmaments,
Set bloods to die,
And starred all purpose with the devil's eye.

Loves, I go to prison for your sake,
Armored from wrong,
Where none but I pays my destruction.
Now be it long or by an atom's luck
Short-shriven, may my life assume the shroud
Of chastity, for when I slept abroad
My ghosts delivered danger in the bed;
Of poverty, for rich I asked return
Double, to glut the beasts I kept; of stern
Obedience, last and dearest. So may I
Listen but once to love,
And all the voices I am trumpet of
Curse God, and die.

SIBYLLINE

The bird in the breast, both eagle and wren,
Cried to the noisy bird in the brain:
Hush your foolish chat, come kill
The sparrow caught in the wind's will,
Or lay your paltry wing on the wind,
Take the sun to strike you blind,
Nourish the fire, and call it kind.

The bird in the brain, both cock and crow,
Sang to the bird in the breast below:
I do not kill my daily food,
All night it runs on river and road,
I pick its tired blood in the sun,
And call harsh benediction
When my black feathers turn to gold.

By those four voices I was killed,
And by the birdless mouth of hell,
In a black-leaved cave I sit and mourn
For battle-weather and birdsong.

MONTMORENCY

When that July, unlike most threatened flames,
Descends in sheer magnificence of corn
Tongues, and the tiger lily's eyes
Answer the rude stare of the cyclops sun,
Then mariners, cool in the cave of dusk,
Survey these acres that the moony mist
Cannot disguise the care of, for the six
Spaced willows in the meadow wet their hair
Precisely where the guided brook sends up
Its silver, and this cedar points the air
Above the tables and the serenade
Like Vincent's trees, that lit the lamps of God.

But we concentrate
On the bugproof candles, now that dinner's gone
To be scraped for the dogs, behind the old facade.
Shall I tell you the horrid thing that Oggie said
When we went to camp? Remember it was
A thousand miles, the taxi after the plane
To Chester, and a dreadful price, I thought,
For that unupholstered jitney, especially when
He fishes half a day for his real living.
Well, anyway, we had to go in a boat
To see the senior life-saving, and Bart
Naturally took his shirt off; it wasn't hot
But there's not much sun in Canada, mostly fog,
Even inland. And do you know what
That child said, practically choking it out to me?
He said, "Please tell Daddy
To put his shirt back on."

Oh, do you raise
Terriers? I never buy a bitch
That doesn't have ten tits. I count them.

Yes, sometimes I pick up a book, but really
In winter it's the car pool every other
Week, and now that Tom is in New York
Three days, it's hard to organize my time.

I drink, much of the night, and go south
In the winter. One could hardly call it waste.
The rain-crow has retired. The nightingale
Does not visit our shores. Out in the years of space
What unnamed birds call music to our lips?
Oh I could speak and die to name one thing
In nature with an accurate name. The ships
Of our salvation throb. Put on your shirt,
Barton. Your hairs will wither at the root,
And all the race step forth as smooth as saints
In danger, or in love with God's own fire
That sings along the gables of this pyre.

ADVENT POEMS, 1963

"The shepherd's brow, fronting forked lightning, owns
The horror and the havoc and the glory
Of it."—G. M. Hopkins

1.

I saw some havoc strike a tree,
And where it fell, a dead man lay.
I saw sick stars and empires all
Shrivel to spots upon a pall.

I heard ghosts breed, and women crack.
The fur flew off the shepherd's back.
He crept on freezing knees to retch
Where naked kings stuck in a ditch.

I grew gigantic eyes to stare
Upon a shrinking insect's bier.
I pulled the knife out of my side,
And ashes greased the floor like blood.

2.

Was this a dream? I left that house
At midnight where the murder was,
And crept on freezing knees to pray
To silence at the blackened tree.
But it grew blacker by my stare,
And burned away my eyes like fire,
And burned the pleasure from my loins,
And labor from my working arms,
And every cry my cold lips sent
Fell down in cinders. And I bent
Where all my guttering treasure lay,
And learned a second way to die.

3.

It is silent under the steeple, cold enough
To crystallize the little light. The dead
Would tremble at that sign: one star, one note.
The stone could melt, the tree leaf: they do not.

The shroud of mourning coats me like a ghost,
And like a ghost, bone-white, I gleam and sing
The folly of warmth and song, and of love most,
And the folly of grave comforting.

I came alone by light into this dark.
I laid the light like tears upon this stone,
Come late, come last to the bitter and difficult
Task: lay all things down.

I laid them all but what I could not spend,
The love that blood created in its lust
For love: my father's feature, the child-hymned
Warm breast, bright wing, one germ alone untarnished
In all that holocaust, one bone to cry.
What shall I cry? I burn in hell? And he:
I burn my child to honor, lest I die.

4.

There is a worse than nothing: loose
The lewd mind from its bloody sheath
And let it plunder heaven and hell,
It cannot bid itself farewell
Until it creep under its skin
And hold its gibbering breath, and drown.

5.

And the glory
Of it? That we will not die?
I walked the orchard in a winter thaw.
The ugly mud turned worms up to the sun,
And stiff mice softened for the harrier's maw.
Oh sparkling boughs! What is not animal
Breaks clean, or burns, or blooms without a will.
Without a will, it startles underground.
Without a will, it crackles in the sky.
Could my heart hear the Appalachian
Dull thunder break, if I lay still as stone

Under Catawba, still as poplar roots?
Still as this branch that stood the pruners' hooks?
Wind hones. Star sharpens. Now it is the time
Our peace, they say, stood up to bear our pain.
I lie down dusty. Father of seed and dream,
And if of mercy, bear me man again.

6.

I walked the wild hills in the still of the year;
No blood but mine beat summer to its eye.
No eye but mine built Blue Ridge from the sea,
Or saw rough Tinker shudder and lie plain.

I have learned my history like other men,
Cracking the ice to see the water move,
Threading the thick brush grown upon the fire,
Conjuring love by all the names of time.

Conjuring one, the Child born over and over,
To be the secret name for the oak's shelter,
The secret name for the hawk's cross in the fur,
The winter rose, the parching head of summer.

In that sweet manger, darkened by the blood
Of beasts and innocent victims of his name,
Did God lie once, to suffer and be born
And weatherbit, under his vane of time?

The hare that has no wishes does not see
The Christmas angels breaking on my eye,
Or Easter wings performing feats of light.
I walk December in the dark and bright
Woods, and I wish, and see no more than he.

7.

And who shall walk the tides of time
And lift the gates of Paradise?
One with swords upon his tongue
Or one with lilies in his eyes?

A heavy blade lay in a tree.
The legend ran: "Who takes me up
Shall fear no other enemy.
I cut the death-worm from the crop.

I spear the moth, I shave the rust.
I scatter every sandy house.
I flatten all the heads of lust.
I blind the little eyes of grass."

A child who could not read came by
And laid his hand upon my hand.
Inseparable, then and now,
We walked away across that land,

And begged at many a battened door,
And sang at many a sun-go-down,
Slept once on sand, and once on flower,
And finally, upon a tomb,

I traced this legend: Season me,
Thou Lord who counts the sparrow's quill.
Raise me in time bloom, bird, or tree,
Unsevered from my blood, thy will.

8.
This was a dream. I drew that sword,
A feather, from the airy wood,
And walked with peace in all my blood.

The grass stood up along my way
The hawk, with pity in his eye,
Fed, phoenix-like, upon his prey.

This was the sword that cut the dream
Of self, the knife at my birth-string.
By blood alone I walk in time,
Weeping and praising.

9.

Now burn, new born in winter's bin,
The hard moon and the stars between
Her rise above the orchard close
And set on Appalachian.

I see at morning with my tears
Burning the pruned and sparkling boughs,
From name to night, from flame to ice,
How little is her turning space.

Oh may this child new born, now burn
The arc of winter with her name,
Night's crescent, and returning day's
White shadow in her lifting eyes.

DANAË

This love I make
Alone, and for my sake,
In a room of the summer town
Where you have never been.
I call his name a god,
His shape gold;
Since the sun cannot fall,
He comes glittering small,
Coining the air bright;
Finches in flight
He may be, or the great
Acacia falling over me.
I am laved
In radiance, each sense clean,
Loud awake in the dream
Where at last I know my name
Is Danaë, Danaë.

Oh when you speak that name,
My love, or one day when the little son
Crawls on his mother's breast, and I cannot tell
Myself from Rachel or Anna at the well,
One day when I chatter over my chores
And the light is late,
If there is a sudden glint
In my eyes, or a softening
Of habit-hard attendance, it is no soft dream,
But that by which I love you, and I am.

A CURIOUS FIRE

A curious fire sang in my bones;
Slow, sometimes, as the crowded sea
Casts fragments of its weedy bronze,
It cast its clownish freight before me.
I could build up Avalon,
Or knock old Troy to ashes, down
Pompeii in cinders, or raise up
Lopsided Chartres, or Sinai's tip.

But sometimes it would crest and hide
All creatures in its dancing. Then
I knew all fires are lit by five
Fingers that hold the match of time
To flesh and bone, and all fires burn.

THE FOOL'S TONGUE

"Tongue, hold! Tongue, hold!" I cried,
And when it would not stop
Raving upon its luck,
I told them how it lied.

From cellar to rooftop,
As it were not my own,
It turned my treasure up,
It knocked my treasure down.

And people came to steal
The coin of such a fool,
And laughed him off the land
With his lying tongue in his hand.

Till wandering by a grave
He cast the traitor in,
And though it could not rave,
Look how the travelling worm
Partook its mysteries,
Till he heard the small birds call
With his own voice from the skies:

"No place, there is no place
To hide the tongue of a fool.
The winds undo its grace
And spread it pole to pole,
Till every luck he had
Is squandered out in air,
And oh, but the birds are glad
For the secrets of that liar!"

A TRIM RECKONING

I could let Honor rot,
Thinking of one proud head
Strumpet Honor brought
To an incestuous bed,
Exacting as her fee
What honest whores despise,
The very mint of the heart
And coin of the eyes,
Till not a beggarwoman,
Borrowed child and all,
Had stew for her dinner,
Or pity for her soul—
Only a day gone hungry,
And Honor's lockers full.

FOR A GOING-OUT

Because you will soon be gone,
And our busy hearts will lie
About the year's return,
And our busy fingers weave
A seemly dress for love,
Let us count peacefully
All we are masters of.

Elm, arcade, walk, and hall
Like laughter fall;
The iron cross goes down.
Eyes not our own,
Nor like our eyes, nor eyes,
Will mock up other skies
With signal passion.
And every man will fail
Whose passion is a pawn.

I live in this belief:
Archaic prayers prevail—
Faith in a cut stone,
Dancing for rainfall,
Goings-out, comings-in.
My loves, I cannot spell
Your passwords up or down,
Your songs in hell,
Your honor, or great pride,
Your name or changed face.
I can only tell
That once, in this place,
Apple-side, mountain-side,
Gray head and golden head,
One could call a man happy
Before he was dead,
In garden, steeple, desk,
Book, candle, or done task,
That made the seasons burn
In love's consuming name.

GARDEN SET

1.

It may be that the best, most blessed love
Is love of nothing. Rude japonica,
You shoot so from the roots, in bronze disguise.
I know you now, my beauty. Bring the shears!
Or all the lawns in Roanoke will die.
I keep the grass, my queen, to see you by.

2.

Chrysanthemums, like words, grow tall too soon.
Down, Jumbo. Down, outrageous Miss Pompon.
Off with your head, Green Jack. Good warriors all,
Grow tough, grow double, practicing the fall.

3.

I have a castle
Three stars high,
   Tarragon and rosemary,
   Sang the garden child.

I have an apple-tree
Two birds thick,
   Pokeweed, lopseed, daisy, dock.
   His eyes were mild.

Fetch me a coverlet
Four leaves thin,
   Lavender and cinnamon,
   To hide my song.

In a pasture wide as sleep
While the singing children make
   Music daylong.

4.

Greystone William at your book,
Come look, come look!

When philosophy is spent
From the caterpillar's tent
Flies the bright moth of the air
Into nowhere.

5.

Two ladies I remember from old songs:
This one that had a garden in her face,
Lily and rose she was, a summer place
Yearlong, a winter dream, lily and rose.

This other was a song or secret breath,
And where she sang, the maple came in leaf,
And where she went, myrtle and violet lay.
Her footstep made a summer. And which way
I care for, music-master, and which way
Is best, madrigal-maker, say, oh say!

6.
Whether the gray sky over us
Listens, whitethroat, hears, chipping one—

Tchap, tchap, tuk, tuk, down dusk, up dawn,
All quick green spaces in between
Made gay—

There is no bird alone
Under the little leaves of the sun.

7.
The gorgeous beetle loved Euphrosyne,
Evangeline loved he, douce Chatillon.
Three red and yellow graces in green weather
Called to the devil and the devil came.

8.
For nothing at all but pleasure, rusty flag
And ragged purple flapper, do you wave?

A man could die in April, with the sky
In ribbons. Rabbi, only the grave would fail.

9.
What more, what more, what more to love,
Light of August, distant dove?

I sing in the throat of a poet who is dead.
I sing because he is dead.
                              Make what you will
Of memory, Earth-Mover, Master Mole.

Let the incredible phlox consume the hedge.
Let Madam Moon fill up the arms of night.

This dark, this light,
This past, this present—
Fie! It is enough.

SUIT

That time I was too proud,
Still decently arrayed,
To beg a coal or rag
Against my winter need.
But you, because you had known
Others come freezing back,
Thought to insure your own
Rich hearth from the weather's knock;
Flattered my strength, my sick
And unconditioned tongue,
And set me ears to win
Seasons beyond your home.

Do you think if you do not bind
My body in some cheap cloth,
That the gaudy stuff of the mind
Will keep me warm enough?
Think what a reed will cure
The desert eye of its tower
And palm-girt pool; what worn
Apple or bitter root
Restores a hungered throat
Better than heart-grown fruit.

I do not ask your treasure.
To refugees and the poor
A crust and a tin of water
Make grace at a rich door.
Let me add such a blessing
To begging love, no more.

A PRAYER FOR PARENTS DAY

Now as they clear the land
And drain the old pond
Of children, lovers, and ducks,
It is not of the frail arks
And feathery mates I think,
But of the abiding still
Stone, when the wave sinks.

Some minister or saint
Decried a sandy house,
Yet Florence owes her glory
To a girl's loveliness,
And circles out of harbor
Serve Dido for address.

Where is the cast flint
By which the circles tend?
I throw the last slight gravel
Into Hollins Pond,
Past fathering. I think
Of quick circumference
And Adam's adamant
That made the waters dance.

And pray foundation
For every rising arc.
A rib of hurt creation
Immortalized that park
Where sycamores fell down
And rains and rages came
Like bulldozers, to shock
The stubborn boundless rock.

THE WINDS

The winds of space, spiced with the latest spring,
Even stinging on the lips like winter's strong
Unstoppered breath, are music. But my song
Stammers and breaks upon the winds of time.
My love, if you were only of this place,
Poor as perhaps it is, and death to face
Soon from the windy skies, still I could play
Notes that would turn black midnight to broad day,
Wounds to excuse for mercy, want to flood,
And pay all favors with my lung-driven blood.
But you go guarded from that tune, wrapped back
In some old concert of a summer night,
Or clash of bells against a freezing noon,
Deaf to the weather where I mark my time,
And time my enemy I cannot sing.

TO WILLIAM WORDSWORTH FROM VERMONT

They laugh, bird-watcher, that you knew
Joy in rock, wood, river, or rainbow,
Or rather that the cliff moved, the night spoke,
The buck stood, and passion broke
The child's first heart. Not I.
I shed my hearts like sailors, growing by
Sunbreak or savor or seeds' press
Into the unsyllabled darkness
That raises all things bright,
Beautiful, fearful, moving, still:
The clouds contending, or the daffodil
That tossed the wandering sun a thousand ways
From English Ullswater.
In joy we start,
And grow by words apart.

On Glastenbury once I saw
The pale moon hesitate, but sky
And earth, divorcing, cast her free
Till cold on Pownal, cold on Bennington,
Her puppet light drained down,
And every eye she praised the valley long
Selected love.
Old puppet of the moon, this mountain night
More sharp with stars and waters than a dream
Of islands conjured in a poet's sight,
Not my eyes bless, but light.

And yet we half create,
As you say. The man has memory,
And quick as Adam's ear or Eve's bare eye
Was fruit and echoes, we are swords and fire,
Cities and song. We come trailing time
Like some old patchwork garment, half our own,
And, improvising fashions, stumble down
The path from chaos and old night. Undear
Things tutor us: not one pure voice
Across a field at evening, but a voice

Counties off, years off, crowds into that call
The sounds of an old summer, locusts in feather
Against a falling house, a ten-years-useless
Barn, the haunt of doves and secrets—all
The freight of sense, held easy, ready to spill
A lowland harvest on this granite hill.
                                        Old Rydal
Reaper of snows and fountains, every crop
Of every season's seedtime pushes up
Its blades to plume the pocked, perennial landscape.
Tintern, or ruinous
Tintagel, caves of Greece
And Cumae, cypresses
Winging the silver night at Arles, or meadows
Of childish May—low mint, lost irises—
Not light, but my eyes bless.

THE SILO UNDER ANGEL'S GAP

The silo under Angel's Gap
Through garland orchards breaks in the morning light.
Forty times by the sun
My eyes have gathered June
And stored a heap of fodder in a bin.

Stalk over stalk, the green turned down to gold:
Whatever beat once on the bloody field,
Or split the roof of air.
Dido is there,
And the rag doll I murdered in the cold.

All mountains shrivel to some sort of food,
Eryx and Andes, Ida, Otter Peaks.
Mad David helps his eyes
To Adam's husbandries.
A tortured Jew translated by the Greeks

Leans out from heaven in pitiless mockery
Of the coarse bread and the raw dreggy wine,
Shadows that fire the gut
Until death puts them out
To feed the shadowy fish and Circe's swine.

I take these shadowy hills to fill my eye.
Shadow on shadow falls till it come night.
Helicon, Everest,
And Woody's barn at last
Ride with the moonless meadow out of sight

Into the fallow dark where blood and dreams
Refashion all the populace of day.
And forty bones that shook
When Eden's summer broke
Rehearse the garland rising in their clay.

THERE WAS A BIRD

Love, I will tell you a tale.
There was a bird sang sweet,
A fabulous nightingale,
Had never a crumb to eat,
Never a bough to ride,
Only a voice, a voice,
That would strike the heart from your side
Out of all histories
Of any month but May,
Any scent but musk,
Till all you could taste was wine
In cool, perpetual dusk.
Listening, you would smile
At heaven already heard,
Then you would ache a while
That you were not that bird,
No, nor that bird's mate
That you might fly with him
And sing at heaven's gate.
And your glad eyes would dim,
And you would taste your tears,
And feel the rise of the sun
Over the quartered years,
And feel your blood run on.

Tomorrow and today,
Every bird on his bough
Has more than heaven to say.
Love, shall I tell you how
Your face was bright, unkissed,
Your house the very land
Where hunger and danger vanished,
Or how your unclaimed hand
Held comfort? Shall I tell
I lost that foolish smile,
Remembered with a sigh
That paradise put by
As it were still to make

For pity, out of the thin
Rafters the winds shake,
Out of the winter moon,
Scant nourishment, full pain
Of labor, calloused skin,
And Graybeard looking in?

Shall I tell how I sing
To the beasts? Or how I pick
A feather for your cap
Out of the frosty patch,
A feather from the wing
Of the jay, maybe, whose blue
Blaze at winter's gate
Makes every bird more bright?

CIRQUE D'HIVER

Could I have been a clown,
A raggedy tumbling man,
To paint my passions on,
Go little, or dress tall,
To tread a giant ball,
Or shed a burning suit,
To whistle a random note
Till all the children shout
At Jocko in the ring—

But no. I truly sing
Without the grace to call
The world and his heart a fool
Whose luck will always mend
For laughing on its end.
And all the children turn
Sick when the stilts burn
And the greasy colors run:
These tatters are my skin.

A BALLAD OF EVE

The blessed worm of Eden sang
At my immortal ear:
The rose will riot on the vine
Year after year;

Night after night in love unbought
The man beside you lie,
And children run on painless feet
Around you day by day;

One god, of all the gods that be,
His table will suffice,
And hand and heart and tongue will know
No enemy but peace.

I walked alone into the dark,
Looking for my deed.
I struck my hand upon a rock
And could not make it bleed.

I lay across the lion's path
Who skirted softly on.
That whole wood was passionless
Up to the edge of dawn.

And there upon the bough it lay,
That made my first heart break.
With human hands I plucked the sky,
With human hunger ate.

And then such plenty was to do,
Danger and pride and pain,
It took me years to fashion true
God's dreaming song again,

The voice that doubled in my ear
Then, in my first of days,
And seasoned love with pity so
I had no tongue for praise,

That now sing back, daylong, the dark,
And nightlong sing the day
I walked the years from paradise
Where god beside me lay.

THE SEASONS

1.

Up, up, great blades. Grow green, you teeth of spring.
By Thebes it was, by Thebes I did my sowing.
The dragon made my apples. Wheat was born
Of his breathing face, and of his feathers, corn.
Shake out your leafy mane, America.
Grow great, Tehuantepec! Kenai, grow green!

2.

It is not a maid and not a mother.
     Sing Persephone.
But yet a wife and yet a daughter
     Asleep under the tree.
May the twelve winds of the sky
Move together quietly,
And the quarreling waters run
So smooth the blackest sands are warm
At the water-lily's root.
Stop the melon, hold the fruit,
Hear the sleeper's heart in dream
Breathe like children: Proserpine.
     Child and queen, Proserpina,
     Light and softest love, stay near.

3.

Run, Master Merlin, Camelot is down.
Gorgon is dead. A city that was not stone
Rose on a harp, a harp of holy air.
Arthur, alas! Alas, proud Guinevere,
And all the pretty swords that kept the hall!
A rubble of proud names, a stony tale.

4.

Taliesin, Taliesin,
Years upon the sea he lay.
Taliesin, Taliesin,
First a man and then a boy,
Sang the letters of the wood,

How the oak and ash were laid
In leafy battle side by side,
Told us how the world began,
First a boy, then a man,
Years he lay beneath the snow.
Taliesin, raise us now.

A JOURNEY

You are always walking away
With the light, bright journeyman.
I wander under the leaves
Of the old town.
The signal hours fall;
Shop, office, hall
Attend, as if the sun
Could never say farewell.
I must make the sun my own.

For the traveller travels well,
Carrying songs to spend,
Branches whose touch can heal,
Seed for new land.
Yet travels heavier
Returning, from the freight
Of foreign syllables,
Beasts crying at night,
Pulses of wind, and hot
Odors that grow
Nerves in the traveller
Where no nerves were.

Now in Virginia
The orange lilies patch
June's raggedy green dress.
Some apples have red rust.
It has all happened before.
What should we be but poor?

The hours answer.
In the central dark
Where we are not loved enough,
Something heavy as gold
Glints by the mineshaft:
The sun in a vein of rock,
Beating mysteriously!
Children at nightwork

Lament the murdered day,
Tremble at what is not
Departure, but a way
Of rising up to walk
When the rock rolls away.

FOR CHRISTMAS, 1960

I think, this winter night,
Child of a crooked house,
Of every path made straight
Across a wilderness.

To Carthage many a one,
Cathay and Darien—
And Palinurus drowned,
And Dido left to mourn,

And Egypt's horse beneath
The crude returning seas,
And Montezuma ruined:
All flights, all entrances.

The scorn of Pharaoh drove;
The acrid cloud on Troy;
Guinevere's, Helen's gold;
Allspice and ivory,

To bones in the Southern Cross,
Cripplings of fire and ice,
Fruited Americas,
And Everest at last.

Old leaves, this winter night,
Shift at the locust's foot,
Random as the hope
Our newest pilgrims take

For city, song, and kin,
For beauty, pride, and lust.
Be with us in the air,
Old sibyl voices. Dust

Can ride the winds of space
To find the mouth of hell,
Birdless as ever, close
As Cumae in the soul;

Or near as Bethlehem,
Across the years of light,
Some harbor for the son
Of man, companioned bright

By stars that never were:
Columbus' lode, or pure
Galahad's spy that drove,
Clear as consuming love,
Through semblance, season, scar,
To manger and to shore.